COUNTRY OF LIGHT

ALSO BY JOSEPH STROUD

In the Sleep of Rivers (Capra Press, 1974)

Signatures (BOA Editions, Ltd., 1982)

Below Cold Mountain (Copper Canyon Press, 1998)

LIMITED EDITIONS

Unzen (Tangram, 2001)

Burning the Years (Tangram, 2002)

COUNTRY
OF LIGHT

poems by

Joseph Stroud

Copper Canyon
Press

Cover art: Marion Patterson, *Wildcat Fall,* Yosemite National Park, c. 1970,
black-and-white photograph, from her book *Grains of Sand,*
Stanford University Press, 2002.

Illustration on page 115: Chen Rong, Chinese, first half of the thirteenth century.
Nine Dragons (detail), Southern Sung dynasty, dated 1244, ink and touches
of red on paper, 18¼ × 431⅝ inches. Museum of Fine Arts, Boston,
Francis Gardner Curtis Fund 17.1697. Photograph copyright 2003
Museum of Fine Arts, Boston.

Author photo: Janine Sprout

Copper Canyon Press is in residence under the auspices of the Centrum
Foundation at Fort Worden State Park in Port Townsend, Washington.
Centrum sponsors artist residencies, education workshops for Washington State
students and teachers, Blues, Jazz, and Fiddle Tunes festivals, classical music
performances, and the Port Townsend Writers' Conference.

LIBRARY OF CONGRESS CATALOGING-IN-PUBLICATION DATA
Stroud, Joseph, 1943–
Country of light / Joseph Stroud.
p. cm.
Includes bibliographical references.
ISBN 1-55659-205-1 (alk. paper)
1. Sierra Nevada (Calif. and Nev.) — Poetry. I. Title.
PS3569.T73C68 2004
811'.54 — DC22
2003023281

3 5 7 9 8 6 4 2

FIRST PRINTING

COPPER CANYON PRESS
Post Office Box 271
Port Townsend, Washington 98368
www.coppercanyonpress.org

for

Sam Scott

&

to the memory of

Roberta McNamara Stroud

Tsuyu no yo wa
tsuyu no yo nagara
sari nagara

ISSA

Contents

3

I Wanted to Paint Paradise

⌧ ⌧ ⌧

4

Passing Through

⌧ ⌧ ⌧

COUNTRY OF LIGHT

I

Plainsong

The Potato

Three days into the journey
I lost the Inca Trail
and scrambled around the Andes
in a growing panic
when on a hillside below snowline
I met a farmer who pointed the way —
Machu Picchu allá, he said.
He knew where I wanted to go.
From my pack I pulled out an orange.
It seemed to catch fire
in that high blue Andean sky.
I gave it to him.
He had been digging in a garden,
turning up clumps of earth,
some odd, misshapen nuggets,
some potatoes.
He handed me one,
a potato the size of the orange
looking as if it had been in the ground
a hundred years,
a potato I carried with me
until at last I stood gazing down
on the Urubamba Valley,
peaks rising out of the jungle into clouds,
and there among the mists
was the Temple of the Sun
and the Lost City of the Incas.
Looking back now, all these years later,
what I remember most,

what matters to me most,
was that farmer, alone on his hillside,
who gave me a potato,
a potato with its peasant face,
its lumps and lunar craters,
a potato that fit perfectly in my hand,
a potato that consoled me as I walked,
told me not to fear,
held me close to the earth,
the potato I put in a pot that night,
the potato I boiled above Machu Picchu,
the patient, gnarled potato
I ate.

Dancing with Machado

Fields of Baeza, I will dream of you
when I can no longer see you!

⊠

Spring has come — nobody knows how.

ANTONIO MACHADO (1875–1939)

What did I know? Baeza was just
a village in Andalucía where I decided
to stop. For I was tired of the road, of trains
and wandering. I remember the river,
the olive groves, and the distant
Sierra de Cazorla. I remember the light
above those mountains. I didn't know
what I was doing in Baeza, I didn't
know what to do with the absence
of love. Every day I walked through
the plaza and the streets, then out
into the fields. One morning I passed
a house, with a plaque on the door —

    ¡Campo de Baeza, soñaré contigo
    cuando no te vea! —
    ANTONIO MACHADO, 1915.

This was Machado's house, this
was where the poet had come to live
after his wife's death, this is where
he wrote his poems of loss — *Lord,*
what I loved most you tore from me.
These were the fields he walked —
a solas con mi sombra y mi pena —

7

where I walked, as well, alone,
with my shadow and my grief,
where I did not have to speak.
What good was my broken Spanish,
what did I have to say? One day
on my walk through the village,
I passed a hall, and heard clapping,
guitars, a loud *staccato,* the sound
of heels stamping on a wooden floor.
Through the doorway I saw a crowd,
and a woman in the center, dancing
flamenco, one arm raised, curved,
swaying like a snake, the other
gathering the ruck of her dress—
on her face a fierce look—pride
or scorn—her heels attacking the floor
as if stamping out grief, loss, memories—
the crowd, the faces, the guitars
nothing to her, dancing somewhere
within herself, making us all
catch fire. And when it was over,
when finally I left, I took the dance
with me, took it past Machado's house,
called out to the old poet, called
for him to join me, took him along
into the fields, through the groves
toward the river. Machado danced
the color of light on the mountains—
I danced the silver of leaves—together
we danced the sun on the river—
just the two of us, two men
dancing alone in the shimmering
fields of Baeza.

The Performance

A cold winter night, three raccoons
in the persimmon tree, three clowns
lurching around, branches sagging,
springing, the whole tree quivering—
at its top, the crown jewel, the last
and best of all persimmons, toward which
one raccoon makes his careful slow way
across a branch, reaches with two hands,
grabs, tugs hard, juggles it, teetering—
the other raccoons watch as this
knucklehead in his confusion lets go
of everything—persimmon, branch,
dignity—flips head over tail,
plunges through branches, snags
a limb, and hangs by his hands—
meanwhile the persimmon hits the ground,
and it's a race to see who can get it—
the smallest scoops it like a football
and begins on three legs to run—
which doesn't work—another
grabs it, loses it to the third, and they all
tumble down the road, the persimmon
bobbling among them like a moon
on fire, as into the night, scrabbling
and careening, they disappear.

First Kiss

was with Sonia in the closet
a summer morning her parents
off to work and the neighbor kids
were playing spin the bottle which
Sonia did and it stopped dead at me
so they pushed us into a closet
and there we were in the dark
muffled among the hanging clothes
nervous excited we didn't know
how to kiss so we just grazed
our lips and clutched each other
before opening the door to our
friends crowding around
as Sonia and I looked down
from our new height as if
we had glimpsed some secret
back there in the dark among
her mother's dresses her father's
stiff trousers something
unspeakable in the bodiless clothes
the empty sleeves and pant legs
dangling and brushing against us
ushering us closer together
in the perfume smell of
her mother the cigarette odor
and English Leather of her father
as Sonia and I grasped and swayed
our eyes shut tight as our mouths

in that first blind groping kiss
among the ghostly limbs clutching
and shuddering around us

In a Lydian Mode

after Cavafy

NORTH BEACH, 1963

We met in Vesuvio's
among the night tribe drifting
from Toscas and City Lights.
I cannot remember her name,
or her room, only our suddenly
open bodies, the yielding,
the crossing over. I cannot
remember what we said after.
In that other time. Waking
to foghorns, mists, streetlights
opalescent through the windows,
those nights like crushed pearls.

HAIGHT-ASHBURY, 1965

A Victorian bathroom, incense
and candles, Erik Satie, hashish,
a bathtub, where I soak, steam rising,
and across from me, leaning back,
Diana, her hair wet, her nipples,
all of time drifting, one silver note
on a piano, and then another,
the *trois gymnopédies,* which will
never end, which will go on
across time, sounding here,
in this place, now, in this body,
this memory making music of me.

Ode to the Smell of Firewood

"Oda al olor de la leña"

PABLO NERUDA

Late, when the stars
open in the cold,
I opened the door.
                    The sea
was galloping
in the night.

Like a hand
from the dark house
arose the intense
perfume
of firewood.
A visible scent
as if the tree
were alive.
As if it still pulsed.
Visible
like a robe.
Visible
like a broken branch.

Overwhelmed
by balsamic
darkness,
I went
inside
the house.

Outside
the points
of heaven were glimmering
like magnetic stones,
and the smell of firewood
touched
my heart
like fingers,
like jasmine,
like memories.

It was not the sharp smell
of pines,
it was not
the cracked skin
of eucalyptus,
nor was it
the green perfume
of vineyards,
but something more secret,
because that fragrance
exists once
only,
once only —
And there, of all that lived in the world,
in my own
house, by night, near the winter sea,
there it was waiting for me —
the smell
of the deepest rose,
the heart cut from the earth —

and something
entered me like a wave
unloosed
from time
and I was lost in my self
when I opened the door
to the night.

Homage to George Mackay Brown

Who had the key to the star and the key to the grave
Who unlocked the runes in the Stones of Brodgar
Who heard the skalds of sun wreck and sea wrack
Who passed through the silver doors of the rain
Carried shipwreck and lark, snowflake and fire
Who cut the thread from the wheel of Morag
And wove Scapa Flow, the Kist, Eynhallow
Wove stars and named them
> *I am the bringer of Dew*
> *I am the Grain of Dust from the Floor of Heaven*
> *I am the Keeper to the Door of Corn*

Who watched a ship of light crossing between islands
The rowing heavy, like lifting oars from honey
Who anchored in the taverns of Hamnavoe
Who walked in the kirkyard among names carved on stones
Who looked into a fresh-cut furrow
And saw a charred ship, oars dragging through ash and skulls
Who cast his net and brought up the little silver brothers
Brought up the cold running of stars
Who—but George Mackay Brown—
A child of time, maker and voyager
Who yoked his words to the ox of Tammag
And plowed the earth into song

The Birdcages of Oaxaca

for Bruce & Saraí Hobson

Every morning the old man set out his birdcages in a corner of the plaza. Intricate cages, beautifully crafted, carved with flowers and unearthly creatures, all of them swirling in color—lime, magenta, *amarillo,* flame—as bright as the finches and warblers within. Some of the cages were so small, so crowded, I wanted the birds released, I wanted to see them fly over the *zócalo,* and keep rising, above the tombs of Monte Albán, above the Valley of Fires. One day among the passing crowds, a young couple stopped to look at the cages. From their *traje,* their village clothes, I could tell they were Zapotec, Cloud People, from Ixtlán, perhaps just married, they seemed so young, so shy. I watched them gaze at the birds. Dear friends, there are moments when we have the chance for a simple act. I thought how I might walk over, introduce myself, offer to buy a cage and bird for them—*Con su permiso, quiero comprar por ustedes…* But how, without intruding, without seeming the rich *extranjero,* without pride or vanity? I hadn't the grace to manage it. I was young, I knew little of how to be. Nor could I imagine clearly enough those mornings, how that couple might wake and look at the cage, listen to the bird, and for a moment believe there might be, even among strangers, a kindness, a sweet charity.

The Old Poets Home

What do you do if you're a poet and you come to that place where
there are no more poems, when the words are all used up for you,
when the muse won't give you the time of day, or night, what do you
do, do you go to the Old Poets Home, sit around with Orpheus and
Homer and all the other silverbacks, Sappho in a bouffant blue-gray
wig sipping sherry, Eliot with his mouth like a prune, and what do they
do there, trade images, recall great lines, complain all day how all the
new poems seem so slick, so enameled, so gussied up, so much *froufrou*
and decoration, such silliness strutting around acting important, or
worse, confessions in the guise of poems, horrors, details of the autopsy,
poems like being run over by the ambulance, and such little ambition,
poems with no scale, no Vision, when will there be a Major Poem they
grouse, a Paradise Lost, an Intimation of Immortality, look how they look
with envy and contempt at all the new metaphors cruising by in sleek
metallic vehicles, boom boxes throbbing with deep heavy basses, every
now and then the carriage of a sonnet squeaking by, reminding them
of the past, of the glory that once was, how language lit up the dark
night of the soul, lit it up with suns and moonlight, with music and
marvels, great visionary leaps, words falling like rain, like snow, like
stars on fire, but now here they all are, in the Old Poets Home, over
there is old blind Milton watching TV in his mind, and here comes Auden
down the hallway in a frayed robe, puffing a cigarette, face as crinkled
as a dried fig, and there's Whitman, beard down to his knees, still work-
ing the crossword of his Leaves, and there's Li Po trying to embrace
the moon in a fishbowl, and Emily upstairs peeking through her key-
hole, Longfellow wandering the halls in tears whispering *Remember me?*
Remember me?, Donne proud and dressed in his shroud, O what a sad
and gloomy and forlorn place this is, but sometimes a few thoughtful,
compassionate young poets will drop by with their groomed and

friendly poems and let us stroke them, pet them, remember how once in our lives the poems frisked for us, barked, ran out ahead, full of energy and joy, looking back, tongue out, happy, looking back with eyes of love for their old masters, those kind and benevolent and sweet old poets.

Book of Horror

THE FREEZE

Look at the garden
look at the honeysuckle
burned black
by the freeze
look how everything green
has been torched
look at the sheath of ice
over the pond
the ghost flames of goldfish
streaking embers of sun
little memories
of how this garden once
seethed with cosmos iris foxglove
now look
a death camp of dead flowers
in one night the killer freeze
like a wrecking ball through a rose window
blossoms
shattered into ice
as if Yamantaka
the Bodhisattva of Wrath
had come down among us
plundering and ravaging
sheathing everything in frost
giving us a glimpse
of the glacial world ahead
an ice planet
drifting around a dead
burned-out star

PAIN

The pain
was too great
for my body
so they slipped me
through a needle
then I was
nowhere
and when I came to
my body was wrapped
as for burial
the light around me
from no source
a man
wearing a mask
stood over me
saying
all has been accomplished
he touched me
from across
an empire
burning
with cones of fire
where a white
gauze of ash
drifted
over the pyre
that was my
body

Book of Psalms

for Mel Tuohey, Linda Kitz, & Fred Levy

PLAINSONG

It got so
quiet
in the cabin
no voices
no music
even birdsong
gone
from the mountain
and with the snows
the silence
deepened
this was where
I lived
was how I came
to hear
what singing
is

WE SHALL BE RELEASED

Every afternoon that autumn
walking across campus
past the conservatory
I heard the soprano
practicing
her voice rising

making its way up the scale
straining to claim each note
weeks of work
of days
growing shorter
darker
storms slamming the campus
the semester staggering
to an end
everyone exhausted
drained
heading out and going home
the campus nearly deserted
but the soprano
still working the scales
when I passed under the trees
the liquidambars on fire
the clouds like great cities
sailing out to sea
and didn't I ascend
with her
my own weariness
and sorrows
dropping away
didn't we rise together
her voice straining
wavering
at the top of its range
almost reaching
almost claiming
that high
free-of-the-body
final note

LITTLE SONG FOR THE TEN THOUSAND
BODHISATTVAS ON THE KITCHEN TABLE

What's going on
with this string of sugar ants
flowing across the table
these miniature
beings
these little flecks
of incarnation
what's the universe
to them
that they inspect it
so carefully
grasping a tiny piece
in their jaws
bearing away each
sugary jewel
of melon
while above them
another being
watches
and what does he know
grasping
his own jeweled
moment
his own little
happiness
making a sound
that sounds like
singing

TO THE LEAST AS TO THE MOST BOW DOWN

All I can manage
this morning
is this little
cluck
of a song
for which
nevertheless
I am
thankful

BROWN TOWHEE

Everyone notices the stoop
of the hawk
the whirling jewel
of the hummingbird
we all love
the mockingbird
filling the yard with music
the low glide of pelicans
cresting waves
tanagers passing through
in the plumes
of tropical flowers
we marvel at the owl
exclaim
over the eagle
even the great ugly condor
riding thermals
above Big Sur
amazes us

with its enormous
grace
but you
little one
common one
brown towhee
no one
notices you
you're just there
in the background
somewhere
undistinguished
unknown
the unseen bird
bird I'm seeing now
looking through
my window
to the winter drizzle
the slums
of the sodden
desolate garden
the only bird
I can see
the only creature
out there
in the dregs of weather
my sweet
little secret
the drab
nondescript
one
and only
brown towhee

THE SUMMER THE SUMMER BURNED DOWN

Years ago
with Sherry
one honey
summer morning
through the orchard
to the charred rooms
the burned-out
farmhouse
where Sherry
showed me
pulling her dress
over her head
and letting it
fall
among the glitter
of broken glass
wasps
buzzing through
the window
crows outside
crackling their
song of black
cinders
the odor of
tarweed
and apricots
peaches too ripe
on the ground
all those summers
ago

Sherry
and the black
ash
of crows
Sherry and apricots
bursting their skins
wasps
charred singing
honey
honey

MEADOWLARKS & HAWKS

A farm road
in the San Joaquin
heading into the red dirt
of the gold country
miles and miles
of fencerows
with meadowlarks
singing on the wires
the song of one
entering the song
of another
all down the road
window open
I hear song
trailing
into song
the road continuing
as far as I can see

and every mile or so
on top
of a telephone pole
sits
a red-tailed hawk
shoulders hunched
turning his slow
iron gaze
over all he claims
of the singing world

THIS OX, THIS BODY

Once more
to plow
through the gold
field of morning
under the weight
of sun
and when the day
is done
to drink from the trough
cold water
brimming
with stars

Rooms

Remembrance belongs to them that were here.

ALKMAN

The stars and the rivers and waves call you back.

PINDAR

For the world must be loved this much
If you're to say "I lived."

HIKMET

What if you could live
in a cowslip's bell. Like Ariel.
Or like the bee who nudges its way inside
and emerges burnished with pollen.
Look—
a hummingbird plunges its head into a blossom
for a taste of nectar. The Lord said—
In my Father's mansion there are many rooms.
Take your pick. All the spirits
grieve for the room we call
body. They want to dwell
among us, they want to taste and see.
It's said Christ entered the room
named *Jesus.* And when that body
was crucified, he cried out—*Father,*
why have you forsaken me? What
if we could live in *this* world? I know
of a field in the San Joaquin with vernal pools,
lupine, owl's clover, poppies.
I know where there's a hive in the live oak

where you can taste wild honey.
Last night my brother told me he was so unhappy
he wanted to die. He would take his life
if he had the strength. Once, years ago,
my brother found a snake on a canyon trail,
a tiny ringneck snake the color
of the earth on one side, the color
of fire on the other. He held it
in his hands. Held it out like a gift.
Like wonder. A small thing, perhaps,
but maybe that memory helps keep him
here. I remember one morning
on the Manikarnika Ghat where the bodies
were burning. I watched
a man step up to a pyre and with a club
break open a skull, scattering
ingots along the banks of the Ganges,
releasing the spirit, it is said, so it might pass
from this collapsing room
to the next. *In my Father's mansion*
there are many rooms. One
I return to often — memory takes me
to a farmhouse surrounded by orchard
in the valley that is called the Pajaro.
I watch the morning light through the windows
as it finds the couple in bed,
two small people asleep in each other's arms —
I watch as he wakes and gazes at her
as I gaze now, at the two of them —
how young we were, how little
we knew of what would happen —
too soon the seasons turn,

to other arms, to other rooms.
The day's on fire! Roethke cried.
But it's raining outside, it's April, the rain's
pelting all the blossoms — still,
Roethke's right — if I look
I see a slow writhing flame nothing
can put out, a fire burning inside
the day, inside the rain, a flame like silk
the bees brush against
inside the flower, the hummingbird's throat
burnished with embers —
the day's on fire! the night's on fire!
all the rooms are burning!
Keats in his death room, feverish, saw a flame
pass from one candle to another,
like a spirit, and to Severn
cried out — *Lift me up — I am dying.*
If you walk in the Roman cemetery
you will find his stone
carved with the words —
Here lies one whose name was writ
in water. He is buried
in a room deeper than time.
I think of Emily's room
as she stood in throe and transport,
in radiance, in the terror
and the cleaving, in the Hour of Lead.
Like Emily, my brother
is not among the members of the Resurrection
untouched by morning, untouched by noon.
My brother can barely live
in his body. In his room. What then
of the rooms in paradise?

When you look out the window
what do you see? I see
a cottonwood beginning to bud, I see
a skeleton higher than a house
that soon will quiver with leaves,
with the green fire of summer. I believe
it is easy to love summer's vast
sumptuous room. But how to love
what can't be imagined? Death's
quantum world, with its rooms
within rooms, with its doors
to nowhere, or elsewhere. How to imagine
my brother's room, a camper shell
on a pickup in the City of Angels
where he drives looking for a place
to park, to spend the night,
where no strangers, no policemen
will rap their knuckles against his shell,
roust him. *Who can be coming*
to the edge of my gates
at this black hour of night?
Last night the sound of an owl
in the cottonwood.
I took a flashlight, shined it
up through the limbs, and there he was—
a great horned owl, looking down
on me. When at last I turned
and walked away, I could feel
his eyes on my back.
You have made me forget
all my sorrows. —Of thee
I stand in awe. In Shay Creek I stood

looking down at an owl, its eyes
being eaten by ants, more ants
seething from its beak, so many
syllables
trying to get at it—
the rooms within, once luminous,
now empty, the light
going out across the stars, they say,
the deep journey back to provenance.
My brother says—*Yes*—he would like
to see once more the stars
of our childhood—deep summer,
when pollen drifted across the lake
turning to gold the blue water at dusk
and we saw for the first time
Orion rise and drift across the night,
his body in flames over the black water.
Journeys and odysseys. Rimbaud's
voyages. His return from Aden,
his *thirteen days of sorrows*, carried ashore
on a stretcher, his knee the size of a gourd—
Where are the treks across mountains,
the rivers and the seas, O Voyager,
O Outcast? On his last morning,
he woke to the brilliant sun
in his room, the sun he loved,
and he cried to his sister—
I am going under the earth, but you,
you will walk in the sun.
Pindar says—*Blessed is he*
who has seen these things
and goes under the ground. He knows

life's end. He knows the empire
given by the god. But what
of the empire managed by men?
What of Nazim Hikmet whose room
for thirteen years was a cell? Who
every night waded in water and pulled nets
out of the sea, the silver fish mixed
with the stars. Who every morning
imagined his execution — *The poplars*
are blooming in Ghazali, but the master
doesn't see the cherries coming. That's why
he worships death. Close your hand —
the daylight inside your palm
is like an apricot. One day the guards
came for him, came to his room,
and brought him outside
for the first time. He was amazed
by how far away the sky was.
While Nazim was in prison, he wrote
Things I Didn't Know I Loved.
He names them — *sun, trees, roads —*
the list is long — *sea, clouds, rain, night.*
What is it, I wonder, I didn't know
I loved? I didn't know how much I loved
my brother in that canyon years ago.
I didn't know how much I loved
the earth and the rivers and the stars,
all those mornings opening
into bright rooms. I didn't know how
love would cross the years
to here — to this place I have prepared
for my brother — this poem,
this room where he may live.

2

Daybook, Nightbook:
Shay Creek

Waking

These mornings
the Steller's jay comes to the railing outside my window,
comes with his impatient songs, his *rasps* and *burrs,* his news
of the new world, and I rise to greet him, I go out to the porch
and place on the rail a crust of bread, and the jay hops and squawks,
happy, I think, and me too when the mystery reveals itself, as it
does these mornings with *chirrs* and *sheks,* the best a jay
can do for singing, and good enough for me
as I wake and look out to the black-
crowned bolt of blue, alive
and squalling with
such brash
joy

Lodestone

I lie in a hammock in the slow hours
of a summer day, summer at last
in the high country, summer in the air,
in the light, in the poems I'm reading,
poems like deep jade pools of snowmelt
under a summer sun, poems like
whorls of agate. There's a drift of pollen
through the forest, sifting through
the pines and cedars, a fine gold powder
drifting like the crushed ash of sunlight.
In the seep on the hillside the first
rein orchids appear, the night-blue larkspur,
leopard lilies. All summer the seep
will blaze with flowers under the flare
of sun over the Sierra. The day turns
around a single shaft of sunlight
through the pines. There's a whisper
of water from Shay Creek,
like the murmuring of voices
from far away, languorous voices,
honey-tongued, voices whispering
of summer, of stillness, the slow sound
of a heat-drowsed summer noon.
A warm wind rises up the canyon,
sways the pines. Clouds drift over.
If my body were the needle of a compass,
it would point dead center into the deep,
invisible lodestone of this murmuring,
immense, summer day.

In the Stream Pavilion

I walk
with Yang Wan-li out of the Sung dynasty
into the meadow below the hot springs.
We stop at Shay Creek, stand on the bank
and look down into a pool, a few trout
motionless in the shade, the water so clear
they hover in air. I tell Yang how I wish
my life were as translucent as Shay Creek,
how I want to follow it up the canyon
to its source, to the high snowfields above
the valley, above the lake, above everything,
up there in the keen air and blaze of sun.
Yang says, *I'm tired of walking. I want to*
lie down, take a nap. And no more poems
about rivers and mountains! He drops
a stone into the pool. *And the next time*
you're at this, put me in the Imperial City,
or better yet, let me drink and be happy
like Li Po, drifting in a boat with only
the moon for company. I close my eyes.
When I open them — Yang is gone —
he's far downstream, where I've put him,
running the rapids standing in his boat,
shouting and laughing, drunk on wine.

Writing in Tongues

All things are holy! Blake claims,
but does that include these leeches,
these detached tongues squirming
in a pond near the hot springs?
If I stick my finger in the water
one of them will grope its way over
and wrap itself around a knuckle.
It has no eyes, has only a slit
for a mouth, has tiny, rasping teeth
that make a clean puncture, painless,
where it will feast on blood, swelling
with a leech happiness—but not
my blood! I slough the leech
from my finger, watch it squirm
back among its brethren, all of them
undulating in a kind of ecstasy, these
Holy Beings, these writing tongues
of Blakean delight.

On What Planet

From Shay Creek, it's a two-hour drive:

- take Hot Springs Road to Markleeville, turn at the Cutthroat
- follow the East Fork of the Carson to the junction
- drive over Monitor and down into Slinkard
- then 395 south through Topaz to Walker
- go east—look for a dirt road coming out of the Sweetwaters
- drop into four-wheel drive
- take it slow, there're ruts and washouts, loose rocks, drop-offs
- when you reach a fork, take the right, ascending the canyon
- in two miles the road dead-ends at Desert Creek

If it's early summer, the banks of the creek will flame with larkspur
    and monkshood
By August they've withered and gone to seed
That's the time to come
Follow the creek a few miles back to its source, a small spring
    below the Sisters
And there you'll find them, in profusion—explorer's gentian
    (*Gentiana calycosa*), summer's last flowers
Go on, kneel down, get up close, peer into one
See how the blossom funnels into darker shades of blue,
    a cloister, speckled with light
It's like looking into a chalice flecked with stars
Then the mind will give a little nudge, and you are there,
    inside the singing, in a luminous alien night

During the Rains

Driving through the rain to Minden this morning, I saw two men walking in a lake that a week ago was pasture, two men ankle deep in the shallows, stringing barbed wire and trying to hammer fence posts into water, one holding a stake, the other with ferocity swinging a maul, horses standing around them, miserable, cattle up to their hocks in water, the Carson plain in flood, fields runneled with gills and freshets, culverts washed out, hillsides loosening, slipping, everything disintegrating, coming apart, the dead bear I found yesterday below Loope Canyon, skeleton unlocking, carcass sodden, dissolving in rain, and now this morning those two men near Minden driving stakes into water, stringing wire across a lake, trying to keep it all in, trying to keep it whole, driving these words into the page, as if this could make the bear stay, as if I could lash the body together, not let anything come apart, dissolve, wash away.

Over the Edge

When I step to the edge and look down, they're just getting out of the smashed pickup. She appears dazed, stunned, and he's trying to pull something out of the cab, gives up, and looks around. A heavy snow is falling. They begin a slow, awkward climb up the forty-foot slope. I start down toward them, kicking footholds in the ice. Halfway, I brace my feet, reach out my hand to his, and pull him up to me. He scrambles past. She's having difficulty. She can't make the few feet between us, so I edge down a little farther until our hands can grasp. But then I begin to slip, and for a moment I think we're both going to lose it, we're going to tumble to the bottom. But we don't. We clutch each other, then crab our way sideways to the top. The wind is blazing ice off of the pass. Cars drift past in the blizzard, eerie faces behind glass peering out. I help the man and woman into my car. They don't say much. He has a gash on his forehead. But they're ok she insists. *We're ok.* You're lucky you're not dead, I'm thinking, wondering what they felt when they hit the ice and swerved over the edge. I crank the heater to high. The windows begin to fog. We're all breathing hard. I catch his eyes in the mirror. He looks away, ashamed, I think, the way he hurried up the slope without her. The woman turns in her seat. She's wiping the blood from his face. *We're going to make it,* she tells him. And we drive into the white heart of the storm.

Scatology

I'm climbing the trail up from Hangman's Bridge
heading into the hilly, open country below Leviathan.
Mostly scrub pine and sage. The dog runs out ahead,
her nose into everything. She halts. I come up
and look down. Old coyote scat. Marie looks around,
howls. We move on. Near the ridge, the earth's been
churned, and there's sheep dung everywhere, pellets
like desiccated *niçoise* olives. She sniffs a few.
Then we reach the head of the canyon and begin
a descent through rabbitbrush and dwarf piñon
to the east fork of the Carson. Suddenly Marie stops
before a mound, a heap, a small hill of bear shit,
still warm, full of berries with black seeds. She's
got her nose right down in it. She turns and stares
back at me with a glassy look, deranged by this
delicious new odor. I glance around, imagining
a bear somewhere near, maybe gazing at me,
or at Marie, who squats near the stack and adds
her own little hillock. Soon we're making tracks,
breaking a new trail down to the river, leaving
three mounds — still steaming — back in the canyon.

The Little Taj

Built the outhouse this summer—
Lundquist, master craftsman, came up
and we hammered it together—
cedar board-and-batten, pine interior,
window in the door facing up the canyon,
stained-glass window high on the back wall,
so when the morning sun shines through
it's like being inside a jewel—
got an oil heater, a bookshelf, footstool,
got one of those new composting toilets—
every six months gives you compost
pure enough to grow carrots in—
come on over and I'll sauté some
with fennel and a dribble of sage honey,
we'll sit on the porch with a glass of wine
and admire the outhouse—
you can see for yourself
why everyone's calling it the Taj Mahal,
best outhouse in all
of Alpine County.

Cutting Down the Jeffrey

Paul Hanning comes over with Bill Reese,
two chain saws, a can of gas, an ax, some wedges,
and we all stand around and look up at the Jeffrey
towering next to the cabin, the Jeffrey that all winter
drops clumps of snow on the chimney, that sways
over the roof when the winds come up — so —
I've made up my mind to take it down, except
I'm not going to chainsaw a hundred-foot pine tree
and have it crash down and split my cabin in half—
so I hire Paul to come and do it. He squints up,
Yup, that's a nasty lean. Where do you want me
to drop it? I point up the hillside, an open space
between a cedar and some white fir. I figure
Paul's going to strap on his spikes and climb,
strip the limbs on the cabin side to shift the weight
of the fall, maybe even set a rope and have Bill
walk up the hillside with a come-along, but Paul
just eyeballs it. *How high you want the stump?*
Then jerks his big Stihl and begins the first cut.
I stand there with Bill, but I'm looking around
for which way I'm heading if this goes wrong.
Halfway through the trunk, Paul eases the bar out
and starts another cut, coming down at an angle,
and in five minutes he's sawed out a thick wedge,
looks like the slice of a watermelon. He walks
around to the cabin side and starts another cut.
Bill jams wedges into the crack, then sledges them
with the maul. The tree quivers, sways, there's a loud
crack, and the Jeffrey comes crushing down,

a huge leg-trembling jolt as it hits the mountainside,
exploding needles, resin and dust, branches
shattering into the air. And there's the tree
on the ground, dead center where I had pointed.
You want me to buck it? Paul asks, then walks
the trunk, whacking limbs with a two-bladed ax.
When he's bucked the tree into rounds,
we stand around, drinking a beer. *Where now?*
I ask Paul. *Up to Poor Boy. Beetles got a lot of trees
up in there. Forest Service wants it thinned.*
You need any cords after this, he laughs, *give a holler.*
When they leave, I gaze at the Jeffrey. It looks
like a shattered spine, like the broken back
of some creature from the Mesozoic, vertebrae
strewn over the hillside. Now no more clumps
of snow on the chimney, no more waking at night
in windstorms waiting to be crushed. Now
there's firewood for two winters, and there's
woodsplitting to be done, the stacking of woodpiles,
there's morning after morning of work to do.
I look at the stump, the shimmering of air above it,
the emptiness, the ghostly absence of what once
was there. The Jeffrey, the great old Jeffrey,
is down.

Wintering

October 11—
Woke this morning to snowfall,
kindled a fire in the woodstove,
made coffee, looked out the window
to white trees and silence. Today
I'll do little. Maybe read a few Masters
from the Sung dynasty, maybe work
on the poem that's been eluding me.
Yesterday I stacked firewood—
incense cedar, Jeffrey, white fir—
lugging them up from the woodpile,
stacking a cord chest high on the porch.
Around noon the weather turned,
clouds streaming in from the west,
and now this morning the first snow.
Yang says, *The mountains are chilled*
by a cold sun. Autumn light trickles
into my poem. I think of the winter
to come, how the sun will walk the ridge,
how light will scale the canyon.
In those months, sealed in,
I'll build fires in the woodstove,
watch the logs seethe to embers.
All winter I'll let the poem burn
within me, tempering each word
in silence, in the winter sun
forging my life, honing my spirit
in the country of light.

Living Alone

> Loveliest of what I leave behind
> is the sunlight
> and loveliest after that the shining stars
> and the moon's face
> but also cucumbers that are ripe
> and pears and apples
>
> PRAXILLA OF SIKYON (C. 450 B.C.)

This morning Praxilla asks me if I know
Han-shan, if I have ever been to Cold Mountain,
do I know the way, could I take her there.
I tell her — this is Shay Creek, we're 6,000 feet
in the Sierra Nevada — in the dead of winter.
Why do you want to leave Sikyon, where pears
ripen in the sun? Why make that long climb
out of the classical world, to follow a trail
disappearing among cliffs and clouds? Even
if you're lucky and able to find Han-shan,
he's just a cranky old hermit who won't say
anything, probably won't even invite you
to sit down. Praxilla sighs. It's hard to live
in this one poem, she says, even if it is full
of sunlight and stars. When you close the book,
I have no other life. So open Han-shan, put me
on Cold Mountain. Besides, you have nothing
better to do, and it's been snowing for days —
you can go with me, we'll both visit Han-shan,
and I bet he'll welcome us, we'll sit and gaze
into his fire, we'll drink green tea, he's been
on that mountain for so long, he too must tire
of living alone, must miss human company.

Homage to the Thief

In snowshoes,
pulling a sled loaded with gear,
I plod my way up to the cabin
and find the door
broken in, a foot of snow
drifting into the kitchen.
A black bear? — that old bachelor
that hung around the canyon
last fall? But a bear with a taste
for Tennessee bourbon,
the whole bottle empty, the top
carefully unscrewed, next to a shot glass
on the kitchen table? And my
buck knife's gone, my compass,
my book of Weston nudes.
Well now. Buddha says
we don't own anything. He's right,
of course, we don't even own
these bodies that walk us over snow,
that break in doors, crumple
pages of poems to build
a fire. There are some who claim
we get to come back in another
body, get to keep coming back
until we get it right. What would
this thief return as? A jackal?
And given my life, what about me?
An ox? A bumblebee?
Dear Thief, thank you

for cutting me loose,
thank you for these thoughts.
Maybe now I'll try to live
another kind of life, maybe I'll even
get lucky, I'll get to come back
as an egret, solitary, standing
long hours in fields, gazing into pools,
no doors, owning nothing, standing
under open sky, now raising
my wings, rising above the river,
flying over the fields at dusk,
now disappearing
into night.

Reading Joyce in Winter

I sit in bed reading "The Dead"
the night of winter solstice
I'm on this side of the world
this side of the seasons
my spirit waiting for dawn to open
the slow opening morning glories
I planted with seeds of fire
before I came to this mountain
before I entered winter
and its days going out like embers
the silence so huge
I can hear snow falling over the Spur
over Burnside and the Hawk
falling across my life
filling the hours the days
where someday I will become
one of the shades
the snow drifting out of the night
lit by the moon as if all the stars
were coming down on fire
drifting through the pines
and falling across Shay Creek
across the Bog of Allen falling
into the dark mutinous Shannon waves
flake by flake the snow
falling faintly through the night
softly falling like the descent
of the last end upon all
the living and the dead

Late Night, Year's End,
Doing the Books with Tu Fu

for Sam Hamill

Ghost fires in the jade palace. Moonlight
a scattering of opals on the river. Over us
beasts of the zodiac march across the night.
We drink cup after cup of warm rice wine.
It's time to take out the ledger, to figure
the year's accounts. Tu Fu, if our days
and nights are the principal, if all the years
are interest, then how much do we owe?
If I subtract my grief from joy, what is left?
Tell me, old friend, how does it balance?
In one of your last poems you talk about
the stars outside your hut, how impossible
to count them. *There are no numbers,*
you say, *for this life. Who cares if we're*
in the red? Or the black? Add a few zeros,
and we're rich. Erase a few, and we're poor.
You're right, Tu Fu. Rich or poor, the night
each night burgeons within us. The mornings
open with sunlight. Why count them?
Instead of numbers, let me enter words
into the ledger, this account of our friendship,
this little poem from me to you, across
the glimmering, innumerable years.

3

I Wanted to Paint Paradise

GIOTTO DI BONDONE
(C. 1266–1337)

In the piazza today at noon everything in a swirl of light. No shadows. No hint of the spirit. All things in their shining forth. Too real. Like angels in the Rose Window with the sun blazing through them. Gianna's grapes on the table as if they had just been created. The poplars on fire. The Arno like quicksilver.

When the bells ring from San Marco, I stop my work. I bow within me. Three times a day, I stop what I am doing, I let the bells fill my body. In the morning the bells are like silver, at noon like gold, in the evening the bells are emeralds. They ring, and they ring. They tell me how to praise — over and over they ring out how to be worthy of the work before me.

This morning on the Via del Cocomero, I was admiring a basket of oranges, when a pig broke loose from a passing drove, knocked over the basket, tried to dash between my legs, and knocked *me* over.

Maestro, are you all right? the vendor asked.
Yes, yes, I laughed.
He was surprised by my humor.
Pigs are very smart, I explained. All these years I've been
   making thousands of lire with their bristles. I've repaid
   them nothing, not even a bowl of swill. So, how can I
   begrudge a little revenge?

And besides, how could I tell him, it was good to be down on the ground a moment. It's true I have painted basilicas in Rome. That some call me a Master. But brother Francis would love this story. To be brought to earth by a pig. To be down among all the other miracles, the oranges scattered about me like small suns, to be astonished once again.

To paint the body accurately is not enough, it must be made to occupy a credible space, not stacked like wood or floating above the world in some mystical suspension. The body must have depth, a dimension that cuts into the space around it. Like sculpture. There must be light and shadows. There must be a logic to the arrangement of figures in their landscape. The old man this morning scything wheat, the oak casting a pool of shadow, and behind them the hills receding farther and farther, diminishing to a point that vanishes. Can this be measured? Music has rules of harmony. Mathematics has its golden numbers. And for painting as well? Are there laws of dimension, of proportion and space? If there are chords of sound, might there be as well harmonies of light?

The dog whimpers in her sleep. She is chasing hares again—her paws scrabble against the floor, her tail twitches. Soon she will wake, and look around. She will come back to this world. I love looking into her eyes. They are amber, like a glass of moscato held up to the sun. I want that color for the dusk in the garden at Gethsemane. Topaz. For my painting of our Lord abandoned and weeping among the flowers.

The crow on Gianna's roof waits for just that moment when the child has turned away, then it drops down and has the crust in its beak and is off over the piazza toward the Baptistery. I think I hear laughter in its *caw*. Or perhaps mockery. The crow in my painting sits on the roof. Watching. It can make no sound. It cannot spread its wings like a miracle. It will never fly.

Taddeo wants to start right away on a massive panel. He wants to paint the Crucifixion. He has a vision of the Resurrection. I want him to learn how to make a brush. To use the soft hairs from Gianna's white hog, not the stiff black hairs from wild boars. I want him to crush burnt almond shells to make a rich black. To grind chicken bones into powder for a primer. (He can find some under the table.) I want to tell him —Before you can paint a panel, you've got to make one. Use the easy wood—poplars, linden, willows. I want to take him into the forest. I know where there's a seep in the hillside. If he scrapes it, he will find seams of many colors—ocher, rose, sinopia. If he wants to paint crowns, he must learn how to hammer gold into a leaf. For his sky, he will have to crush lapis lazuli. If he wants to paint Paradise, he must first find a pig.

The Pope wants me to come to Avignon. Visconti wants me in Milan. Every week a new summons, a new commission—paint this, paint that —flattery, money, huge blank walls only Giotto can manage, they say, come, Maestro di Firenze! Taddeo is miserable with ambition. He would paint them all. And more. Fame is a sickness in him. Nothing can fill him up. Even my sweet Maso is tempted by it all. Maso who is just now mastering the touch of joy on the human face. Who one day will learn the touch of grief. I am tired. Everywhere great cathedrals are rising. All this overreaching. This arch higher than the last. In Beauvais they say the choir will disappear in the clouds. What will hold it up? I remember the valley of Mugello, the stable in the Colle di Romagnano when I was a boy. The mud walls flecked with straw. Dirt floor. Roof beam sagging. I remember those nights in summer I would sleep out there. The dawn through cracks in the ceiling. The little hen huddled over her eggs in the corner, the secret nest my mother hadn't found. Our burro looking down on me as I woke on my straw bed. Looking down with her calm, sad eyes. No paintings. No banquets. No ambition. No pride. A world as simple as the Lord's childhood. Yes, brother Francis, I hear you. I was just a peasant boy. I knew nothing. I didn't even know how happy I was.

Gianna knows everything in the neighborhood. She knows everyone's secret life. Even more than the priest. Father Arnolfo is a kind old man. Too kind, too innocent. Something like you, brother Francis. At Confession, the people do not wish to disappoint him. But Gianna. She knows *all* our sins. Even before we commit them! And her memory is long. Does she forgive us? Who can tell. But like many others, I have longed for absolution with my head on her lap.

Every day I see the three blind men begging in the piazza near the Duomo. To be blind. My greatest fear. As you say, brother Francis, we should confront our fears. So, I practice it from time to time. I close my eyes. I touch the table. I pick up objects. I let my hands explain. I break open the pomegranate. I imagine jewels. I touch the walls of my fresco. How poor, how blind my paintings are. Eyes closed, I see how they might shine. I see a world lit from within. I see my poverty.

This afternoon, returning from a walk, I stopped on a hillside and looked down on the Arno. It was dusk, the river filling with the melt of sun, shimmering, like the long swirling tail of a dragon. I suddenly became dizzy. My body felt far away. I saw a star fall from the sky. There appeared a woman clothed with the sun, the moon under her feet, upon her head a crown of stars. I saw a dragon rise out of the river. There was war in the heavens. Michael and his angels fought the dragon, and it was cast out. It fell upon the Earth, as starlight, as sunlight, as hail and fire mingled with blood. And the Earth opened. I saw the Duomo come apart, crumble into the pit. I heard a voice crying *woe* to the inhabitors of Earth. I beheld a pale horse, and he who sat on him was Death. The sun became black and the moon became as blood. Every mountain was moved out of its place. The Kings of the Earth hid themselves in caves and said unto the mountains, Fall on us, hide us from the face of Him that sits on the throne, for the great day of His wrath has come. And I beheld a great multitude, who stood before the throne, before the Lamb. They were clothed in garments of the sun, crying with a loud voice — Blessing and glory and wisdom and thanksgiving be unto our God. That is what I saw. It lasted an instant. It lasted a lifetime. Then I was back, looking down on the Ponte Vecchio, the little boats on the Arno, the Duomo in the distance. I turned and walked back down into the city of men.

The sun on the Arno, calm water, a reflection of the Ponte Vecchio, mirror of the two worlds. And now a boat, a man rowing upriver, the oars scooping sunlight, breaking the water into gold. People come from everywhere to see the work of Cimabue. Duccio. They come even to see Giotto. How amazed they are at the frescoes. What miracles, they say, what magnificence. And every night the true night showers them with diamonds. And every morning the sun spills gold into the Arno.

Maso asks me about the burros, why they appear so often in my paintings. I tell him of my childhood in Mugello, my few years of schooling, how difficult reading was, how impossible to make numbers make sense, my great shame as the slow one, the dense one, the one who drew pictures on walls. I tell him of our burro, my boyhood companion, the one who listened to my sad stories with his sad eyes. Yes, I have painted him often. You will see him bearing our Lord as He enters Jerusalem. And he is also there before the crib at the Nativity, the first of all creatures for the Infant to see.

How ambitious Taddeo is, and how impatient. I remember how it was. I remember working for Cimabue, my master. Let me do this scene, I would say, let me paint Joseph's face, let me put rubies in the angel's wing, let me… let me… Cimabue would frown—*Today you work on feet, just the feet of the crowd. And be sure to count all the toes!* One morning he left the workshop. I don't know what got in me. He had been working on a panel—Joachim among the shepherds. I went up to it, and I painted a fly on the cheek of one of the shepherds—delicate, perfectly detailed, a marvelous fly. That afternoon when Cimabue returned, I watched as he went back to work, saw him stop, try to brush away the fly, once, twice, before he realized my prank, my audacity, my skill. I was young, what did I know. He might have been enraged, he was the great Cimabue, this was a panel he had been working on for weeks. He looked over at me. *Come here, Giotto.* And I approached, waiting now for his wrath. But he laughed. *Very good,* he roared, he clapped my shoulder. *Nicely done, Giotto. A good lesson for me. And now a lesson for you —erase it, make the fly disappear, make it so no one can ever tell it was there.*

From the hills above Florence you can look down and see fields, orchards, the Arno, the Cathedral, streets, houses. From above how simple and ordered it appears, as if part of a great plan. From up here there is no Gianna, no Maso, no oranges in the marketplace, no lamentation from the churchyard. From this distance the piazza is without life, no sounds of argument, no laughter, no bells. From up here, away from it all, among the light and the sky and the quiet, a world we can look down from, but where we cannot live.

Taddeo insists the Florentine painters are better than the Sienese. It is not an issue that interests me. When I look at Guido and Duccio, the masters of Siena, I see *più bella che si può* — as beautiful as possible — an exquisite beauty, sensual, charming. Among the Florentines there is perhaps less exaggeration, something more vigorous, serious. The Sienese serve beauty. The Florentines seek truth. One is not better than the other. There are many paths.

No one is allowed inside the courtyard of Giovanni di Fiesole. Often I have walked before it, have wondered what it is like inside. Everyone knows of his wealth. We have heard rumors of his collection, mosaics from Byzantium, bronze jars from the Orient, pottery painted with fantastic animals, silk brocades of paradisal colors, a stone lion older than the Pantheon. Giovanni hoards it all. It is just as well. We pass by his house with our minds on fire, imagining wonders, while he sits in there, alone, surrounded with ashes.

Benedict XI wanted to make Saint Peter's the most glorious church in all Christendom. He sent agents throughout Umbria, Tuscany, Firenze, Ravenna—to seek out the finest craftsmen, the best artists. One came to Florence, came to my workshop, asked for a sample of my talents to bring back to the Pope. I laid out a parchment, dipped a brush in red paint, and drew a perfect circle. Take this to His Holiness, I said. The agent was outraged. This is a mockery, he sneered, am I to have no other design but this? When Benedict received it, I am told, he clapped his hands. He smiled. Bring me Giotto, he said. And thus with a single stroke I entered Rome.

One day the Can Grande della Scala summoned me to Verona. To his magnificent court — musicians, poets, scholars, artists. Dante had passed through, had recommended me. And so I came. And so I witnessed a man with power, who commanded the lives of people, whose wealth was astonishing, a man of large sympathies, much learning, who loved the arts. But also a man of cruelty, greed, a man who ravaged other cities, ruthless, a man who wished to build an empire. And what did he want of Giotto? He wished me to paint. Not a massive fresco, not a biblical scene. He desired that I paint — *him* — life-size, exact in every detail, a kind of painting never done before. And so I began. I had him sit for me. An hour every day when his time permitted. I worked in silence, and listened to him talk. Politics. Strategies. Intrigues. I remember his anger at the feud of two important families, the Montecchi and the Cappellati, a rivalry that threatened to spill over into public carnage, disrupt his rule of the city. He would speak to me of these matters as I made his portrait, as I brought him to life on a wood panel, something for his vanity, that his visage would be known through time, for all to stand before and marvel, his power so great that even Death must bow before him, must kneel down.

I must confess a secret. I have placed myself in one of my paintings. No one will ever notice. It's one of the panels in the Arena Chapel, the one showing the Lord, surrounded by disciples, entering Jerusalem on a burro. In the background, away from the crowd, there is an olive tree, and in it a boy is climbing out on a branch. He is high in the tree, leaning out. He will not fall. He is just a peasant boy. All he wants is to see.

So, what do you think?

Book Title: ....

Comments: ....

....

....

....

Can we quote you on that? ☐ yes ☐ no

Copper Canyon Press seeks to build the awareness of, appreciation of, and audience for a wide range of emerging and established American poets, as well as poetry in translation from many of the world's cultures, classical and contemporary. To receive our catalog, send us this postage-paid card or email your contact information to poetry@coppercanyonpress.org

NAME: ....

ADDRESS: ....

CITY: ....

STATE: .... ZIP: ....

EMAIL: ....

COPPER
CANYON
PRESS

www.coppercanyonpress.org

BUSINESS REPLY MAIL

FIRST-CLASS MAIL   PERMIT NO. 43   PORT TOWNSEND WA

POSTAGE WILL BE PAID BY ADDRESSEE

Copper Canyon Press
Post Office Box 271
Port Townsend, WA 98368-9931

This morning, two ravens in the piazza. Two shadows. The fountain. Fresh cream with strawberries. I can hear the plainsong of monks in the chapel of San Marco. Today I am going to paint the face of our Lord down from the cross. Today I must paint the dead Christ. Yes, brother Francis, I will put you among the disciples around the body, among those grieving—the one looking down whose face is streaming tears. For the weeping Veronica, I will use Angelina whose son was crushed by an ox. For Joseph, I will use Pascual the cabinetmaker as he stood over the grave of his wife and newborn. I will make him an old man. For a flower, I turn to the flower. For the faces of sorrow, I need only look within, open the Book of Grief, where all of us have our stories.

Taddeo has been telling me about the fruit trees in his new painting, how perfect they are, how their fruit will last for hundreds of years, better than the originals, he says, that fall to earth, that perish. Sometimes, Taddeo, I believe you're an idiot. You'd rather paint a plum than eat one.

On the Vespignano road, many years ago, two old men with switches trailing a white ox lumbering through sunlight and through shadows on a Tuscan summer day. Who appear here now, on this wall I am painting, in this church beside the graveyard where they are buried, and where the white ox lumbers on through the country of light.

Yes, brother Francis, I wanted to paint Paradise, a great city, a city structured like music. But look at this rosemary on my table. The bowl of grapes. A cup of water. The iridescent feather of the quill I am using. The stone wall outside my door, wild basil growing in the cracks. The smell of geraniums. The lizard sunning itself on a stone, bobbing up and down with happiness. The blue door to Gianna's house across the yard. Her rooster with his bloodred comb. The bells of Santa Croce and the bells of San Marco and the bells of Santa Maria Novella. The sparrows Maso scatters when he walks from the stable. A puddle brimming with light. The lake above Fiesole, full of sun all day, filled with starfall at night.

4

Passing Through

Sleeper, Awake

                       Look—
a web strung from the lamp, moths
entombed in silk, suspended
in air, and nestled against the shade
a spider, eyes glittering
like distant stars—

                       The Gates
are burning. The City's on fire.
The Body collapses in ash. Neither song,
nor poem, nor any honeycomb of joy,
O Sleeper, shall be your coin
of passage.

Altair and Vega
Crossing the River of Heaven

Who hasn't desired a celestial love?
The *Man'yōshū* gives us Weaver Girl
and Shepherd Boy, heavenly lovers
coming together one night each year.
Hitomaro, weeping, could not sweep
all the leaves falling on his wife's grave.

Swath

Over there in the ditch, rank with vetch
and scarlet runner, tarweed, seeds blistering
in the heat, that's where it begins, that's where
we come apart in our great bed, stripping clothes
from our bodies, spilling cries under the sweep
and threshing arc of the scythe.

Iris

After Lennon died, Melissa planted bulbs.
When they come up, when they bloom,
she said, *you'll think of him.* But mostly
I remember her, Melissa, who comes back
at strange moments, a presence, like those iris
rising as blue flames out of the earth.

Cathedral

I put the shell down and wait for the snail
to emerge. I have much to learn of patience.
I no longer wonder where did love go,
or why the nights are so long. Issa says
the words will find a way across the page,
they will make a path into morning.

Memory: Quonset Hut,
Rodger Young Village, 1947

My mother stands next to the gas heater
in her nightdress—which suddenly catches fire,
quick bright flames rippling, unpeeling her gown,
as my father slaps at her, smothers her in his arms,
the two of them swaying there together, embracing
for the first and only time I can remember.

In My Father's Mansion
There Are Many Rooms

But what about that small room
down the hall, the one with the sign—
Do not disturb—the room my mother
went into, my father, only yesterday
it seems, the room where the door locked
from within, the dead bolt sliding shut.

Reading Wallace Stevens

I close the book and look out the window
up the hillside from the cabin where a stag
and two does pass through the sunlight
and through shadows between the pines,
disappearing among the colors they are,
appearing among the colors they are not.

If Only the Dreamer
Could Change the Dream

Bly asked me if I had seen Logan recently.
No, I said, surprised, *John died... he's dead.*
Bly gave me one of his owlish looks. *In dreams,*
he asked, *has he visited you in your dreams?*
No, I said. John and I were friends in this life.
And I miss him. I miss him even in my dreams.

The Executions on Príncipe Pío Hill

I stand before the Goya in the Prado,
so close all I can see is paint, but if I step back,
a scene appears—men against a wall, soldiers
aiming rifles—so I keep stepping back—
across an ocean, across time, backing away,
hoping it will focus into something I can bear.

Closing This Year's Anthology, I Think of Radulfus Glaber, Who Sought Refuge

and peace from the monks at St. Germain d'Auxerre,
and they took him in, gave him soup, a straw pallet,
allowed him to stay, and for his service assigned him
a hammer and chisel to wander among the graves
of the Brethren, recarving the scarred inscriptions,
chiseling the worn names deeper into stone.

My Lord What a Morning
When the Stars Begin to Fall

I wake before dawn, and sense my house
around me, its skeleton of fir I framed
years ago, back in the time when I believed
I could make a shelter, back in my pride,
when I boxed out a skylight so I might
watch the stars cross over me each night.

Coat of Many Colors

Death is sewing buttons, the coat
is nearly done, soon I will put on
that robe of fire, I'll wrap myself
in the sun, then all the words will blaze,
and scatter into ash, when I become
undone, when I am no one.

Elsewhere

My father picks up my brothers and me at the swimming pool. He is angry and smells of gin. We get in the car. No one speaks. He drives back to the wedding party to get my mother. An aunt takes me aside, puts her hands on my shoulders— "Your father is a good man. Remember this. Sometimes we don't mean to do the things we do." In the car, my mother sits up front. Against her cheek she holds a towel wrapped around ice. We drive across the hot L.A. Basin. We are on the freeway, among the other cars with families inside. We are all driving, from somewhere, to somewhere else.

☒ ☒ ☒

I pick up the phone and it's a woman's voice. She wants to speak with my father. I go back to the dinner table. My brothers drink their milk. My mother looks at her plate. I wait for my father to come back. Our dog is asleep under the table. His name is *Fury*. When my father sits down, he's wearing a face. We go back to eating. Then we're in the den. With our first TV. We all sit before it. No one gets up to change to a new channel. From the night outside, our window glows like a screen. If you were to look in, you would see what appears to be a family.

My Marriage with Death

Death joins me for breakfast at the hotel café.
He orders *huevos rancheros,* lights a cigarette,
gazes at me a moment, then opens the newspaper.
So. One of those no conversation mornings.
We're in the sixth year of our marriage,
vacationing here in the Yucatán, an ancient culture
he knows well. I've been reading the guidebook
about the pyramids, the steep stairs to the altar,
a priest holding up to the sun a fresh pulsing heart.
I watch Death smoke and read the paper, purse his lips,
flicking ashes over his plate smeared with yolk.
I try remembering those first months of courtship,
the walks along Point Lobos, restaurants and concerts,
afternoons in Napa driving through the wine country.
My friends had warned me. Beware this older man.
This man with money and manners, with patience
and culture, a hint of cruelty like a fine cologne.
I wanted it. He made clear for me my presence
in time, how my life surrounds the moment. Even
this moment, this glass of ice water on the table,
dazzling, beaded with diamonds of light. We have
no plans for today. I'll read by the pool. Death
will be off somewhere, as usual. I no longer ask him
about it. Tonight perhaps we'll make love. I'll sit
in bed and comb my hair, the one thing that still
interests him, the only thing left that makes him sad.

Rune

after the Anglo-Saxon

Traveler

        stop

before this stone

        with its honeycomb

under the earth

        Take warning

Don't be

        too happy

The odor will rise

        the Furies will

smell it

        will be on you

like bees

        Of your joy

they'll make

        their honey

as they did

        of mine

in my summer

        my time

in the place

        where you

now stand

Stitching the Woe Shirt

in memoriam:
Kelly Stroud

Inconsolable

☒

As if a word could name it

☒

As if sorrow were an ax

☒

As if a prophet opening the body could read the future

☒

As if a god reached in and scattered her across time

☒

Inconsolable

☒

As if *grief* and *anguish* and *desolation* were threads

☒

As if this poem were a needle

The Death of Lorca

Because you have died forever,
like all the dead of the Earth,
like all the dead who are forgotten
in a heap of lifeless dogs.

FEDERICO GARCÍA LORCA

The Black Squad of the Falangists arrested Lorca. They took him from Granada to Víznar in the Sierra de Alfacar. He spent the night in the Villa Concha. By then he knew he was to be executed in the morning. He wanted Confession, but the priest, who attended the other prisoners, had already left. The guard, José Jover Tripaldi, told the terrified poet—*If you ask God's forgiveness, your sins will be forgiven.* Lorca could only remember parts of prayers, a few phrases from his childhood. At dawn, a schoolteacher, two anarchist bullfighters, and Lorca were walked toward the Fuente Grande. They could hear the sound of water from the spring the Arabs called Ainadamar—the fountain of tears. Lorca knew by heart the medieval poem of Abū'l-Barakāt al Balafīqī—

> *At Ainadamar the birds sing*
> *as great as musicians*
> *in the Sultan's court.*
> *Their song opens in me*
> *that place I entered in my youth,*
> *where the women,*
> *the moons of that world,*
> *beautiful as Joseph,*
> *made every Believer*
> *abandon his faith*
> *for love.*

The four men were shot beside an olive grove. Lorca did not die from the first fusillade. He had to be finished with a coup de grâce. Juan Luis Trescastro boasted in a taverna that he had been part of the squad, that he had finished Lorca off—*with two bullets in the ass for being queer.* An hour after the executions, the gravedigger arrived. He recognized the two bullfighters, observed that the third man had a wooden leg, and the fourth wore a loose tie—*you know, the sort that artists wear.* He buried the bodies in a trench, one on top of another, in no particular order.

Into the Dragon

Tanh and I are on Highway 1 north of Hué,
driving into the DMZ, a stretch of road
the French called *la rue sans joie,*
the wasteland we're passing was once
Quang Tri, the entire town obliterated,
wiped off the planet in 1972.
We cross the 17th Parallel, the old line
between North and South Vietnam,
the DMZ stretching all the way to Laos—
once the most ravaged place on Earth,
in ten years two million tons of bombs,
and napalm, and Agent Orange.
We pass a Land Rover, a group of Brits
clearing mines and unexploded ordnance.
At a beach on the South China Sea
we come to the Vinh Moc Tunnels,
where a whole village lived underground,
the planes passing overhead, unaware.
Then we drive west on Highway 9
over a section of the Ho Chi Minh Trail,
to Khe Sanh, scene of the fiercest siege
of the war—General Westmoreland's *Niagara,*
where the bombs fell endlessly, one airstrike
every five minutes, for nine weeks.
Of Khe Sanh, little is left, a strip of ground
that was the landing field. A battered hangar
serves as a museum commemorating the siege.
There's a logbook with entries from Americans
who were soldiers, who have come back.

One entry reads: *Good men died here fighting*
the Evil that is Communism. 500 Americans
lost their lives in those nine weeks. Someone else
has made an entry on another page, with an arrow
pointing back: *Good men died here fighting*
the Evil that is Capitalism. 10,000 Vietnamese
died in those weeks. One of them was the father
of Tanh, who looks at the photos on the walls,
some showing the area before the war, the jungle
and rice paddies, the jagged range of mountains
running north-south, nearly the length
of the country, what the Vietnamese call
the Dragon's Back. Gradually the land
is recovering around Khe Sanh.
They're growing coffee in the hills.
On a trail in the area a sign warns —
Danger! Stay on path! UXO!
I walk the center, exactly aware
of where I place each step,
when a kid comes tumbling out of the bush,
his hands holding what look like old coins,
tarnished silver, they're dog tags, he says,
authentic, he'll sell them, along with
M16 shells, some of them live.
From his rucksack he pulls out a grenade
and offers it to me, the pin still in it.
I hold it in my hand, and stand there,
looking down on Highway 9 switchbacking
out of the hills, a logging truck gearing down,
loaded with illegal, freshly cut timber
from Laos, last of the old-growth forests
in this part of Asia. Tanh takes the grenade

from my hand. *No good,* he says,
and gives it back to the boy.
On our return, we stop at a Bru village,
hill people, impoverished, desolate, a few
wooden houses on stilts, some old women
smoking pipes, chickens scratching in the dirt,
scribbles that look like words, numbers,
entries in a logbook, about good men,
evil, about body counts, how empty
the numbers are, how real
the bodies were, and I hear
a high-pitched screaming, as if someone
is being murdered, and under one
of the houses I see three men holding down
a pig, its front and back legs tied with rope.
One of the men swings a stone hammer
down on the pig's skull, stunning it.
He slits the throat, draining the blood
into bowls, then cuts open the body,
and the men reach inside, feeling around,
pulling out entrails. Tanh watches me
watch. I think he wants me to say
something. About the day. About
this place. Maybe about my country.
Something about people, good people,
people without blood on their hands,
if there are any, if they exist, and where
might that be, in this life, this brief
journey, this dragon world?

What He Told Me in Phôngsali

Passport? Man, forget about your passport, you're not going to need a passport up there, the only way in is by jeep, then upriver by boat, from there you have to walk two maybe three days, it's in the Triangle, you know, bandit country, guerrillas, opium fields, no-man's-land, no borders, you can't tell if you're in Laos, Burma, China, Thailand, Vietnam, nobody knows and nobody cares, all kinds of hill tribes, Black Hmong, Flower Hmong, Mien, Akha, Lahu, hell, languages nobody understands, animists, weird voodoo stuff, they eat dogs up there, strip the skin from live snakes, milk the blood into a bowl and drink it, some'll even drink the venom, no lie, up there even the kids are on the pipe, look like skeletons, men hunt bush pigs with AK-47s, you better not walk anywhere off the trails, the Americans dropped tons of ordnance up in there, B-52s that couldn't unload over Nam just dumped it all up there, a lot of it didn't go off, people get blown up all the time, you'll see farmers walking around without a leg or missing an arm, it's the dead end of the world up in there, spooky, they say there's still cloud leopards in the mountains, last year they found a new kind of deer, about the size of a dog, barks like one too, got black gibbons, fox bats, gorals, pit vipers, king cobra, got leeches the size of a buffalo's tongue, got dengue fever, liver flukes, lungworms, got hepatitis A, B, C, D, *and* E, malaria, typhoid, cholera, rabies, got Japanese B encephalitis, mosquitoes carry it, a virus, eats away the brain, they say the first symptom is visions, transcendence, like you're waking inside the Diamond Sutra, they got *everything* up there, so I'm telling you you won't need your passport, and don't tell them you're American, say you're Canadian, oh yeah, be sure to tell them you're a poet, they love poets, can't get enough poets up there, they have poets for lunch, and if you get in a bad fix, which guaranteed you will, you can tell them you know me, but if I were you — no *way* would I go up there — OK?

Speaking in Tongues

Lord Buddha, what an impossible language!
Every day I work through the phrase book—

Chào ông/bà	Hello
Có khoe không?	How are you?
Tên là gì?	What is your name?
Tên tôi là Joe	My name is Joe

But no book prepares you for the six tones
of Vietnamese—mid-level, low falling, low rising,
high broken, high rising, low broken—each
a different meaning:

ma	ghost
má	mother
mà	which
mạ	rice seedling
mả	tomb
mã	horse

So—
at the restaurant this afternoon in Da Nang
I try out my Vietnamese. I want to say—
I'd like some stir-fried vegetables and rice—
Cho tôi xin môt rau xào các loại với cơm—
The girl taking my order can't believe
what she's just heard, she can't keep
a straight face, slaps a hand over her mouth
and rushes to the kitchen, where soon

there are loud cackles, hoots, screeches—
then a face appears from behind the curtain,
maybe the cook, an old woman looking
around for this fool who just said something
impossible, unbelievable—who knows
what I said. I settle for a bowl of *phở*
and sit looking out at the road, the sun
filtering through dust, across the way
in a rice paddy, a kid sleeping, sprawled
along the back of a water buffalo, dead
to the world. Behind him, in the distance,
the Cat Tooth Mountains, and the ruins
of My Son, the lost kingdom of Champa,
nothing but rubble now, crumbling towers,
stelae, the stone face of Shiva emerging
from jungle and shadows, lingams
pocked with bullet holes, bomb craters
filled with water, choking with lotus.
I eat my soup, and go over the rising tones,
the falling tones—

mạ	seedlings
ma	ghosts
mả	tombs
mã	horses
má	mothers

ma má mả
like the cries of a child, the elemental sound
in all tongues. I wonder what is the sound here
for *sorrow*, what syllables in this tongue for
forgive us—forgive us the terror we made—

the slaughter—horses of fire howling
out of napalm, the million tombs we left behind,
ghosts of mothers and fathers and children.
From the kitchen I still hear laughter
and the chatter in a language I will never know.
The old woman comes out once more,
a tiny, hunched crone, her teeth blackened
in the old way, comes out and watches me
eating soup. Who knows how many
of her family died in the war. Who knows
what she makes of me. She stands there
with her black smile. Then gives me a sound,
a word, in English, maybe the only one
she knows, one simple sound as I raise
the bowl to my mouth—

  Good

           she says.
I place the bowl on the table
and look at her. I nod, and answer—

  Yes Good

And then in her tongue—

  Vâng Tốt

Passing Through

Hoi An—the Thanh Binh Hotel,
a cheap, grotty room. Fever,
night sweats, tongue swollen,
eels squirming in my belly,
no strength to get out of bed.
What is wrong with me?
Is this *it?* Is *this* the final passage?
For two days I look up at the fan,
three blades slicing the air.
I watch the two geckos
upside down on the ceiling.
Their golden eyes never close.
On the third day they tell me their names,
Li Po and Tu Fu.
They write poems across the walls.
The blades swish over them
and in the *thish thish thish*
I can almost hear Li Po
reciting the *Tao Te Ching.*
There's a sign on the wall next to my bed—
motorbikes firearms explosives stinking things
even prostitutes not allowed in room.
On the fourth morning I rise,
stand under the shower and let the water
stream over me.
On the fifth day I walk
down Le Loi to the Cam Nam Bridge,
past the old Chinese assembly halls,
their roofs carved with dragons.

Near an empty courtyard
a boy stands under a flame tree
holding a string whose other end
is tied around the thorax of an insect,
a blue-green metallic-sheened beetle
the size of a hummingbird
buzzing in slow circles around the boy's head.
From the bridge I watch fishermen
cast their nets over the Thu Bon River,
draw them in, and spill onto the beach
a thousand glittering coins.
I look to the other shore
where coming toward me
riding over the bridge on bicycles
a procession of schoolgirls
all dressed in white silk *ao dai*s
holding white parasols over their heads
floating over the slow-moving waters
like a vision of the white orchids of paradise
in the dream of a dying man.

At the Well of Heavenly Clarity

I was lost in Hanoi's Old Quarter, wandering among its maze of lanes and alleys, the Street of Knives, the Street of Graves, the Street of Silk. An old man noticed my confusion, a stooped old man, wispy beard, beret, who tapped his cane over to me. He spoke a little French, I had my phrase book, and we tried to work out where I was, where I might be going. I opened the map, pointed to the Lake of the Returned Sword, then to the Temple of Literature. Between them—a labyrinth of lines and incomprehensible words. The old man put his finger to a place on the map, then pointed down to the street where we stood. Gradually he traced a route, faced me in the right direction, and soon I was entering the gate of Van Mieu, the Temple of Literature, a thousand years ago the center of learning in Vietnam. The grounds are arranged to suggest Confucian thought. Five Courtyards reflect the elements of human nature, the path through them the Middle Way, the Golden Mean. The grounds were peaceful, quiet, a place of serenity at the center of a seething city. I had been reading about Confucius, Khong Tu, his emphasis on order, selflessness, nonviolence. For weeks I had been wandering through the past, through old wounds, battlefields, graveyards. I thought of the war tales I had heard, the story of the farmer, a suspected VC, who was taken up in a helicopter, held a thousand feet above the earth to terrify a confession from him, then let go over his village. The story of Hué, and its mass graves of civilians the VC left behind. The blood on my hands. On everyone's. I walked the grounds, and came at last to Thien Quang Tinh, the Well of Heavenly Clarity. I looked down a long time, the sky reflected in the water. A long silky contrail passed through the clouds and lily pads, a 747, streaking toward Beijing. Not long ago the contrails were B-52s, sketching murderous, terrifying sentences across the heavens. I looked into the well, thinking of the old man on the Street of No Name. I thought of the map of the heart, the maze, the words we need to translate, from every tongue. Not the political words, but the human, the words for comrade and friend, sister, brother. I looked into the well, a few bubbles bubbling up, and then, rising from the depths, breaking the surface, a turtle, an ancient turtle, moss-backed, eyes a clouded jade, so old, so venerable looking it could have been the embodied spirit of Khong Tu, living here for a thousand years. It stretched out its neck, turned its slow, ponderous head, its beaklike mouth appearing to smile, a smile of heavenly disinterest. It turned its head a moment, looking around at the world, then sank back into the well.

Country of Clouds

Her name is Yeem,
she's a fifteen-year-old Black Hmong,
and we're in a Russian jeep climbing a road
in the mountains outside of Sa Pa.

Yeem is singing the lyrics to Bob Marley's
No Woman No Cry.
She can sing it in Vietnamese.
She can sing it in French.

We are on our way to Ban Khoang,
a remote Red Dao village
near the border
where China crossed over in '79,

200,000 soldiers
would teach Vietnam a lesson,
and two weeks later
180,000 crossed back.

The mountains are in clouds,
a fine mist — *The breath of the dragon,*
Yeem says, and I ask her
Have you ever seen one?

She laughs, but when she was a child
she saw a cloud leopard below Fan Si Pan.
We reach a washout in the road
and the driver slows the jeep.

Yeem says something to him in Hmong
and he grunts,
shifts into compound low,
and we begin a steep climb,

the road no longer a road,
just ruts and a hacked tunnel through the jungle.
In an hour we come to a clearing
blocked off by poles of bamboo,

looks like a tollgate, there's a small hut—
A group of soldiers standing around
armed with AK-47s
and not pleased to see us.

Yeem gets out of the jeep
and begins talking to an officer,
a small man in tan uniform.
She gestures back at me

and the officer shakes his head,
an emphatic *No*.
He walks over and looks at me,
says something to Yeem in Vietnamese.

He wants to see your passport, she says.
I don't have it with me,
tell him it's back at Cat Cat.
She speaks to him.

The soldiers stand around,
curious, watching, no smiles.

Yeem gets into the jeep.
We go back, she says.

The driver smiles.
On the way down
she tries to tell me.
There's trouble with the hill tribes,

the Hmong, the Dao, the Zay.
In the Central Highlands there's been fighting,
maybe the beginnings of revolution,
tribal people and government forces.

She doesn't go into details.
Masking her face,
she looks away.
I don't ask questions.

We come out under the clouds
and drive the main road
toward Lai Chau Pass,
the terraced fields far below

glimmering with water
which make me think
of the ponds in the Red River Valley
on the train up from Hanoi.

Why so many, I mused then,
and it was Yeem who told me
they were bomb craters,
reminders of the American War.

We stop at the Pass
and walk up a slope
through a heavy mist
to a mound of earth on top.

At first I think it's a grave
like others I've seen in villages
but it's not.
It's a gun placement,

the ruins of a turret
overlooking Dien Bien Phu,
where the French parachuted in
and then had no way out.

Ho Chi Minh came through here
after thirty years of exile,
carrying his typewriter,
beginning the Liberation.

Yeem wants me to see
something else,
so we climb higher
until at last we come out

into a country of light
above the clouds,
the peaks of the Annamites
rising out of the mists

all down the length of Vietnam,
peak after peak

jutting out of the clouds.
From up here you can see

above everything, Yeem says.
I come here sometimes.
It's like having a clear mind.
We linger, then descend

back into the mists, into the world
where all we can see is each other
and the trail disappearing ahead
in the breath of the dragon.

NOTES & ACKNOWLEDGMENTS

Tsuyu no yo wa... (page vii)

> Only a world of dew
> this world of dew —
> and yet... and yet

Dancing with Machado (page 7)

Antonio Machado, along with Juan Ramón Jiménez and Miguel de Unamuno, is considered a founder of modern poetry in Spain. When Leonor, his wife, died, Machado moved to Baeza, where he taught school and lived a solitary life for many years.

In a Lydian Mode (page 12)

"Trois Gymnopédies": three piano pieces composed by Erik Satie (1866–1925).

Ode to the Smell of Firewood (page 13)

A translation of Pablo Neruda's "Oda al olor de la leña," from his *Odas elementales*.

Homage to George Mackay Brown (page 16)

A cento, in parts, for George Mackay Brown (1921–1996), the poet from the Orkney Islands.

Rooms (page 30)

"Who can be coming to the edge of my gates at this black hour of night?" — Apollodoros.

"You have made me forget all of my sorrows" — Alkaios.

"Of thee I stand in awe" — Alkman.

"Thirteen days of sorrows... Where are the treks..." — Rimbaud.

"The poplars are blooming..." — Hikmet.

In the Stream Pavilion (page 41)

Yang Wan-li, Chinese poet from the Sung dynasty, a garrulous companion in the high country, particularly in the Jonathan Chaves translation: *Heaven My Blanket, Earth My Pillow* (Weatherhill).

On What Planet (page 43)

The title is from Kenneth Rexroth, who knew the way.

I Wanted to Paint Paradise (page 57)

Giotto di Bondone, commonly known as Giotto, was the master Italian painter of the fourteenth century. Though the iconography of his frescoes is Christian, the spirit that infuses his work is a deep sympathy for the human condition, which he depicted with a realism, candor, and depth of feeling that had not been realized by the painters before him. In Giotto we find the beginnings of a humanism that would become one of the distinguishing marks of the Renaissance.

brother Francis: Francis of Assisi, canonized in 1228, was the subject of many of Giotto's paintings.

Taddeo & Maso: Taddeo Gaddi and Maso di Banco were disciples of Giotto who went on to become significant painters in Florence.

Cimabue: Cenni di Pepo, better known as Cimabue ("oxhead") because of his stubborn pride, was considered the greatest painter of Florence prior to Giotto. According to legend, Cimabue came upon the young Giotto herding sheep and sketching pictures on rocks, recognized his talent, and took him as an apprentice.

Duccio: Duccio di Buoninsegna, the greatest painter from Siena, a master of the older Gothic style, and a contemporary of Giotto.

Can Grande della Scala: the portrait Giotto made of him has not survived.

Arena Chapel: also called the Scrovegni Chapel. Site of Giotto's great masterpiece, a fresco cycle of forty paintings. After seven hundred years (and nearby aerial bombings in WWII), it still stands in the city of Padua and may be visited today. One of the world's sacred places.

Altair and Vega Crossing the River of Heaven (page 86)

Altair and Vega, the brightest stars in the constellations Aquila and Lyra, which come into conjunction one night in the year, are known as Weaver Girl and Shepherd Boy in Japan, and are the subject of many love poems. Kakinomoto no Hitomaro, one of Japan's greatest poets, lived in the seventh century.

The Death of Lorca (page 96)

See *Federico García Lorca: A Life* by Ian Gibson (Pantheon), and *García Lorca* by Edwin Honig (New Directions). Lorca's grave has never been found.

Into the Dragon (page 98)

Though I traveled through much of Southeast Asia in the 1970s and '80s, it wasn't until 2001 that I made my first trip into Vietnam, twenty-six years after the war.

"DMZ": demilitarized zone, a 10-km-wide zone running east-west along the Ben Hai River, dividing the northern Democratic Republic of Vietnam from the southern Republic of Vietnam. It was the most savage battle zone in the war. "UXO": unexploded ordnance; it's been estimated that up to 30 percent of the ordnance dropped in the DMZ failed to detonate. Since the end of the war, 9,000 civilians, mostly farmers and children, have been killed or maimed when coming into contact with UXO.

Country of Clouds (page 109)

Fan Si Pan is the highest mountain in Vietnam.

Gratitude, *always,* to Ellen and Sam and Charis and Rachel. I am indebted to Kirby Wilkins, Dennis Morton, Michael Wiegers, Len Anderson, and especially Rachel Harris for their careful reading and advice. Thanks also to Willis Barnstone, Phil Dow, Dan & Alice Harper, Diana Heberger, Dick & Sue Lundquist, Dr. T. Marshall, Bev Mitchell, Jerry Reddan, Steve Simpson, Bill Siverly, Jerry & Janine Sprout, and the good people at Copper Canyon.

ABOUT THE AUTHOR

Joseph Stroud was born in 1943. He is the author of
four books of poetry. He divides his time between a
house in Santa Cruz on the California coast and a
cabin at Shay Creek on the east side of the Sierra
Nevada.

*Copper Canyon Press wishes to acknowledge the support of
Lannan Foundation in funding the publication and distribution
of exceptional literary works.*

LANNAN LITERARY SELECTIONS 2004

Marvin Bell, *Rampant*

Cyrus Cassells, *More Than Peace and Cypresses*

Ben Lerner, *The Lichtenberg Figures*

Joseph Stroud, *Country of Light*

Eleanor Rand Wilner, *The Girl with Bees in Her Hair*

LANNAN LITERARY SELECTIONS 2000–2003

John Balaban, *Spring Essence:
The Poetry of Hồ Xuân Hương*

Hayden Carruth, *Doctor Jazz*

Norman Dubie, *The Mercy Seat:
Collected & New Poems, 1967–2001*

Sascha Feinstein, *Misterioso*

James Galvin, *X: Poems*

Jim Harrison, *The Shape of the Journey:
New and Collected Poems*

Maxine Kumin, *Always Beginning:
Essays on a Life in Poetry*

Antonio Machado, *Border of a Dream:
Selected Poems,* translated by
Willis Barnstone

W.S. Merwin, *The First Four
Books of Poems*

Cesare Pavese, *Disaffections:
Complete Poems 1930–1950,*
translated by Geoffrey Brock

Antonio Porchia, *Voices,*
translated by W.S. Merwin

Kenneth Rexroth, *The Complete Poems
of Kenneth Rexroth,* edited by Sam
Hamill and Bradford Morrow

Alberto Ríos, *The Smallest Muscle
in the Human Body*

Theodore Roethke, *On Poetry & Craft*

Ann Stanford, *Holding Our Own:
The Selected Poems of Ann Stanford,*
edited by Maxine Scates and
David Trinidad

Ruth Stone, *In the Next Galaxy*

Rabindranath Tagore, *The Lover of God,*
translated by Tony K. Stewart and
Chase Twichell

*Reversible Monuments: Contemporary
Mexican Poetry,* edited by Mónica de la
Torre and Michael Wiegers

César Vallejo, *The Black Heralds,* translated
by Rebecca Seiferle

C.D. Wright, *Steal Away: Selected and
New Poems*

For more on the Lannan Literary Selections, visit:

www.coppercanyonpress.org

The Chinese character for poetry is made up of two parts: "word" and "temple."
It also serves as pressmark for Copper Canyon Press.

Founded in 1972, Copper Canyon Press remains dedicated to publishing poetry
exclusively, from Nobel laureates to new and emerging authors.
The Press thrives with the generous patronage of readers, writers, booksellers,
librarians, teachers, students, and funders—everyone who
shares the conviction that poetry invigorates the language
and sharpens our appreciation of the world.

THE ALLEN FOUNDATION *for* THE ARTS

Lannan

NATIONAL
ENDOWMENT
FOR THE ARTS

PUBLISHERS' CIRCLE

The Allen Foundation for The Arts
Lannan Foundation
National Endowment for the Arts

EDITORS' CIRCLE

The Breneman Jaech Foundation
Cynthia Hartwig and Tom Booster
Washington State Arts Commission

The Board and Staff express
gratitude to

PETER LEWIS

for his years of generous dedication
to Copper Canyon Press.

For information and catalogs:

COPPER CANYON PRESS
Post Office Box 271
Port Townsend, Washington 98368
360/385-4925
www.coppercanyonpress.org

This book is set in Dante with display type set in Adobe Jenson. Each face is inspired by type cut in fifteenth-century Venice, then a flourishing publishing center. Adobe Jenson is modeled after type by Nicolas Jenson, while Dante echoes the faces of Francesco Griffo. Since both faces are products of the twentieth century, they are informed by contemporary technologies and sensibilities. Dante was designed in 1954 by Giovanni Mardersteig and cut in metal for foundry composition. Over the years it has been reworked by Monotype for machine and digital composition. Adobe Jenson was designed for digital composition by Robert Slimbach in 1995. Book design and composition by Valerie Brewster, Scribe Typography. Printed on archival-quality Glattfelter Author's Text at McNaughton & Gunn.